Typescenes.

by Rodney A. Brown.

Unlikely Books
www.UnlikelyStories.org
New Orleans, Louisiana

Unlikely Books
www.UnlikelyStories.org
New Orleans, Louisiana

Typescenes.

by Rodney A. Brown.

Foreword.
by Jonathan J. Detrixhe, Ph.D.

What follows is a mere thought experiment. It is not meant to express the whole, the best, or even a very useful or important approach to the poet and the poems. Now, that being said:

A word is coming up. A word the poet is about to make special. To the extent that, if you immerse yourself in these poems, you will never experience this word in the same way again. And yet it is a common word. Well, not for long.

I want to talk about the poet and the poems without using this word. I don't want to ruin the surprise! Also, this word belongs to the poet now. Of all the things on the lists that follow—from gravestone inscriptions to chair covers to big black dicks to footstep sounds to the blood of Jesus – this is the one thing the poet allows as a self-possession. To my mind, the poet earned it. It belongs in the poet's mouth now. I dare not utter it here.

So that is one challenge I set for myself: I shall discuss the word but shall not speak the word. The other challenge I set is to identify the *enactment*.

This is a special word in contemporary psychoanalysis. It means that, try as they might, the analyst and patient cannot help but recreate, repeat, *enact* the patient's trauma in the process of the therapy itself. The enactment may arrive subtly or explode. The enactment may caress and tickle or peel off faces. The enactment may hide in the room like a cobweb for years and never be noticed, or it may rise up from the floor a chain-clanking ghost to scare everyone shitless. The enactment is like the negative opposite of safety lights on a vehicle; the enactment is built to make sure everyone crashes. The enactment welds shut the hatch on the space capsule; there is no escape.

When you learn the poet's special word, you will quickly see, I think, that you have been ushered in to recreate, repeat, enact. And if you do, which you must do—no escape, remember—you will then do that thing that everything and everyone in the poems have done to the poet. Enact the word. And then you will join the poet's list. Which includes everything already. And everything flowing in one direction. Now you, too. You will become aware of your always-already presence on the poet's list. Only now you are swept up, flowing in that one direction. You will ___ the poet.

Nope, you can't avoid it. Merely by arriving and venturing in, you will be doing it. Doing it to the poet. No, I'm sorry. Even should you determine to be very careful, to tread lightly, to be humble, to only listen, to mind your p's and q's, to pay your respects, you will ___ and so become a line item in the poet's eternal accounting. For what the poet has created here is indeed that entire, that complete. The *singularity* of the poet's commitment to the word seals your fate.

Now let me explain what I mean by "the singularity of the poet's commitment to the word," even while still trying not to use the word. Again, the surprise of the word is important. I don't want to spoil its entrance! And this is the poet's word now, remember—to the extent that I realize I am deep in an abomination zone just by touching it in this way. The enactment is full on right now.

And you are watching me do it. I am ___ the poet. But that being said:

To say that the poet's use of the word creates a persistent theme would be a gross understatement. To say that it casts a spell gets closer. To say that the poet wields the word like a black hole wields gravity, then we might have it. So harken, reader:

Get ready to enter a universe collapsing on an atomic point. Where the compass has only one heading. A gravity well infinity deep. A piano falls through space, crashes down, and plays only that one chord. That incredible chord. *Onggggg!* Eighty-eight keys but only one chord. Thus a monolith. A monad. A singularity. Just like trauma.

The word.

Everything is coming in. No choice. Beyond porous: because there is no saturation limit. Beyond open: because there is no lid, I imagine it was torn off. Beyond receptive, beyond penetration, beyond rupture: because there are no edges to the orifice. Not a wish to contain all but an actual containing of all. For example, the poet's will to manifest this singularity is so strong, the word can contain both matter and antimatter: "doubt" and "faithfulness" (p. 8), "lack" and "gain" (p. 11), "empathy and critical judgement" (p. 20).

And we watch with growing horror as the word calls into being things that shouldn't exist or at least come resplendent in pain: "___ your own child," "open someone else's mouth," "___ the thought that meat are negros" (p. 35).

How could anyone have learned to do such a thing? And do it so well? Command a word in this manner, to this degree? I think we know the answer. But as soon as we venture to say, to add our understanding, interpretation, reaction, this also becomes part of the poet's list, part of the poet's trauma. We ___. And our presence retraumatizes.

To realize this may feel like the end of the world. But it is actually only the beginning of the power of these poems, just as an enactment is always the beginning of the therapy. And because of the poet's commitment, nondefensiveness, complete openness to the process, the monadologic of trauma and the unidirectionality of the word are eventually spun up and melted down into a surprising new substance, unexpected here in the poet's singularity: a pluralism.

At this peak of agency, trauma becomes learning. The uninvited are welcomed. The unidirectionality loops around on itself. So a pluralism made of the singularity of trauma, which is a miracle broad enough to include our enactment, our ___, and maybe even forgive us in advance, thus inviting us to rise to the poet's occasion.

I hesitate to add "and forgive ourselves." There isn't a happy ending like that here. I believe in the process described above—healing derived from a commitment to self-disclosure and openness, so that the singularity of trauma becomes a pluralistic or multidimensional experience replete with pain but also learning—but this is no panacea. In real life, it only works sometimes, and then only for some time. And no one is ever free from recriminations, including the poet, who also ___ us.

Indeed there is an incredible alchemy of good-will-to-power at work here where shit turns into gold. But gold in an honest system is still pretty shitty. From the poet we get self-overcoming on a massive scale, but we also get the torture chamber in which the training for mastery took place. Unforgettable, even if everyone moves on to a more comfortable place. This is no katabasis, far from it, but this is also no Christmas eve. There's *Amor Fati* here, but also a plainspoken certainty that none of these things should ever have happened.

All in all, the poet remains committed to the word and perhaps thus masters the trauma again with each reader that comes along. Yet I believe the poet somehow still reserves the space to tell us to fuck off if we're not getting it right. That is how far the poet has come with the word. The poet can also wield its opposite.

Publisher's Preface.
by Jonathan Penton.

The first thing you need to know about *Typescenes* is that you can dance to it. Martin Mull is said to have coined the dismissive aphorism, "writing about music is like dancing about architecture." Many beautiful minds continue to write about music, but fewer have the nerve to dance to other art forms, despite the fact that a glorious building, like a profound work of literature, is worth dancing about. Fewer still have the nerve to create a non-musical work designed for dancing. *Typescenes* is such a work; some thirty-nine pages of dense language about which, as the founder of The Brown Dance Project, our Author has danced; about which our Author has invited others to dance. One such dance can be seen at https://www.typescenes.com/immediate-dances-score-3/.

This might be new to some readers, but our Author is versed in the intersection of text and dance. We refer you to our Author's translation of the POA Module on HIV Education into dance. The POA Module on HIV Education, developed by Nesha Z. Haniff, is a method to raise HIV awareness in low-literate populations; it is highly accessible public health information. Dr. Haniff has encouraged translations of the Module into various spoken languages; it did not occur to her that our Author would translate the Module into dance. But in 2014 in New Delhi, our Author performed h(is)er choreography of the Module. This remarkable, and ultimately pedagogically useful, translation can be examined at https://bdpmodule.wixsite.com/bdpmodule. I would suggest this work—the communication through dance of public health information—directly informs *Typescenes*.

The second thing you need to know about *Typescenes* is that it is necessarily a treatise on American Black male mental health. While our Author's own gender identity is fluid and playful, (s)he is well-versed in the traumas experienced by American Black men. In this sense, *Typescenes* is not only an accompaniment to our Author's choreographic work, but a continuation of it; it, like the Author's translation of the Module, is public health information. To be clear, this treatise is poetic. Like the choreography of *Typescenes*, the simple reading of *Typescenes* requires, as Dr. Detrixhe says in his Foreword, an active collaboration between our Author and you, our Reader. The knowledge in *Typescenes* cannot be simply "banked" in the Freireian sense, but must be engaged with. Through this engagement, our Author's treatise can be understood and valued as a medical text.

The third thing you need to know about *Typescenes* is that it is a collection of prose poems that can and should be read for experiential pleasure. Originally a single scroll, the poet Annie Finch worked with our Author to create its current form, a brief literary collection. Although it requires engagement, *Typescenes* requires no poetic education; it is immediately accessible and enjoyable as art, beautifully presented and thematically relevant to casual and committed readers. Put another way: you can still enjoy it if you proceed to page 1 and skip all this stuff in the front.

Unlikely Books is a publisher of the arts, and it is thus with pleasure and pride that we note that our Author trusted us with this multifaceted manuscript. It is in this spirit of pleasure and excitement that we bring it to you, Reader, in the hopes that you will receive its extensive offerings. We believe it deserves multiple readings, and we can't wait for you to experience it as we do.

Acknowledgements.

Thanksgiving to everyone! Trademark of
the book *Acknowledgements* section has
generally been some listing of helpers
and support. In such proximity where
people besides the Author are coming in
contact with the Author's crafting of
language. For certain, Reader reading
Author's bookwork out in the world as a
publication. Theoretically that moment
of contact being, Reader becoming the
other present in relationship with the
Author by way of Reader meeting the
Author's language. What might it suggest
that everyone be in this together?

In Acknowledgements some histories of
listing are familiar. The Author's
God, other life instructors like
adversaries, academic and informal
educators. The publication and bookpress
staff, earlier publishers including
communities the Author has not chosen,
are biological, and who've also been
instrumental in the Author realizing
their book project; albeit inspiring
so much as to earn their name printed
on some Author's manuscript page space
somewhere. Pervasive too, the Author's
life partner garnering some specific
mention. Acknowledging them being
there in particular ways. Then there
are always influences the Author knows
but can not list by name or should not

name or refuse to say out loud. So much
to unpack. Considering the context
of Passenger or being with in this
manuscript. Each of us deserves our
sincere gratefulness. Have it, here.

About the Author.

do hybrid_ form_ performance_ an installation
series reading_ reckoning_ and soaking up ruptures
or spill_rbrown8 explains_ "_the problem_s_
to be solved suggest that through interpreting
various artistic forms_ that intentional creative
practice will continue to be ways of safety_" Her
projection_consciousness global_
–Rodney A_ Brown Performance Matter artist
biography Bronx Academy of Arts and Dance
*(BAAD) Saturday 11 April 4pm 2020_*

About the Author can be discerned by
analysis of their experimentation and
the products they devise_ For example_
in much the same way Langston Hughes
explores aspects of Black life and
socialization_education in Mother to
Son_ writing_my life ain't been no
crystal stair_(Hughes_ 1922)_ Perhaps it
is because this Author was born in the
Appalachian mountain system tagged *two*
*for one*_ nigga(er) and fag(got) (DDm_
2019)_ that this Author composes from
social circumstances _our own tumultuous
and revolutionary age (Orwell_ 1946) _
he(r) subject matter being determined by
their queer_and times s(he) lives in_

Primarily this Author's scholarship
is Community Engaged Learning through

artmaking_ Their work tends to deal with
how Black primary source perspectives
describe short-term possibilities_
immediate self-sustainable alternatives_
and_or ways of speculating far beyond
or collective futures_ One example_
this Author's recent New York City
performances "Making Health Information
Accessable with Dance Composition"
initiated a project in progress that
translates a constantly evolving oral
HIV teacher training practice (Haniff_
Nesha Z_) into a movement based form
(Ma with Brown_ 2015)_ An additional
path of that process artwork includes
text performance and choreography that
illustrates Pre-exposure prophylaxis
(PrEP)_ Daily PrEP to Prevent HIV_ and
a Hepatitis C Virus health education
training specifically designed for peer
outreach to special needs and homeless
populations_ These multidisciplinary
creative process projects are also an
example of how this Author imagines
artwork as a manner of fugitivity fleeing
from intolerable circumstances_

That this Author was reared
conscientized (Freire_ 1970) in a
particular way_ and grade school
educated in the geological terrain
literally marking division between slave
or free peoples during the Civil War
period_the Mason and Dixon line_the Ohio
River borderlining northern territories

from Confederate south and other America
sectors form large swatches of the
Ordavician pieces they are of_

The about of this Author is the
plurality of these and other proximity
relations_ Thus these relationships
are also deep inside this Author_
especially how physical_ social and
psychological component parts of Black
living_which when read together create
some singular convent of Blackness_out
of which narrative repetitions of Black-
lived experiences (oral histories become
folktales are poems as typescenes) can
be analyzed_and then arranged into
something of a singular pre-eminent
creative project that is an otherwise
doing-for-ourselves now_ and [enactment
with] one another now_ what no one has
ever done for us_ (Hemphill_ 1993)_

Since this Author grew up being held
up and also having to hold themselves
down while colliding with separate and
unequal educational and social service
systems_ waves of culturally ignorant
national drug policies on crack and
opioid epidemics_ United States Veterans
lives_ Black bodies with AIDS_ Black
bodies on Black bodies violence_ federal
surveillance of poor and woke bodies_
especially legalized brutality including
government legislation leading to the
murder and forced migrations of peoples_
This author knows miracles_

Author's Theoretical Foundations.

Bronx Academy of Arts and Dance (BAAD)
Virtually BAAD Festivals Archive:
www_baadbronx_org/2020-baad-ass-women---
boogie-down-dance-festivals-archive_html

Langston Hughes, "Mother to Son" (1922)

DDm, "Fly On The Wall" from album *Beautiful Gowns* (2019)

George Orwell, "Why I Write" (1946)

Haniff, Nesha Z., "Pedagogy of Action: Attempting to Transform Ourselves and Our World Through the Process of Teaching a Simple Oral HIV Module," University of Michigan, Ann Arbor, Michigan

Brown, Rodney A. with Ma Mansi, "Module Manual: A Guide to Choreographing the POA Oral HIV Prevention Education Method" (2015)

Paulo Freire, *Pedagogy of the Oppressed* (1970)

Author's Preface.

[Much of Mississippi's (Ohio's) and the South's (America's) past is characterized by increased resistance to white supremacy in the face of overt and subtle racism that resulted in multiple crimes. These include crimes against the body, crimes against property, the collusion of public and private institutions in preventing access and opportunity to all people and conspiracies of silence that continue today.]
I/We am typescene(s)
Know us individually
As a collect.

—From *Turn Me Loose The Unghosting of Medgar Evers Poems By Frank X Walker*

Contents of this manuscript were
developed overtime allowing the Author
to digest stress and rehabilitation,
focusing on the physical body in motion
(ambling running improvised dancing,
wiggling, shaking, rocking, nodding,
etc…)in conjunction with poetry on the
page. Yes. I, the Author, got issues.
Inside this understanding I situate this
manuscript action as an ecosystem for
somatic activism, language and theory
I am employing to express a physical

practice in conjunction with various
fields of studies and experience.

To be read out loud.

Enter an outlet. Enter a few tools.
Enter a practicum of therapy. Prayer,
rituals, and meditations enter as an
approach for us all to lean in, and take
good care.

Enter shields or garments Black people
can put on for survival. Outlining one
pursuit to understand trauma, discover
how to arrive at what is really needed,
and perhaps recover whatever we can of
the things we've ever lost or had to
literally (or otherwise) leave behind.
This art is a practice of organizing
picture perfect situations that operate
as environmental messes needing to be
cleaned up. Messes that leave human
bodies, so it was with John Crawford
III, laying down in the aisle at a
Walmart store in the state of Ohio;
Dead. Messes of tiny spots of blood on
Connecticut toilet seats and bright
cloth material.

Enter questions asking what is
happening?

Pointing out warning signs that there
is something opened, leaking, broken,
perhaps even an emergency. In this

manuscript the choreographerauthor's
emergency is a single voice in a large
constellation of voicestories held
together by Black Americans' primary
source legacy of living through trauma.
A piece of autobiography. A perspective
in Black life. Typescene(s) of Black
living. Perhaps already so familiar
to the audience. Either way, and in
this conscious, a singular manuscript
emerges. One that builds on (and
extends beyond)legacies of self help
book writing, prose poetry genre, and
durational performance(s) while choosing
to take advantage of Shange's choreopoem
model. Making the choice also to bend
and reimagine what has been done to get
at what is needed in this 21st Century
time—Is this an app that you are reading
on a phone?

This Black American mental
health project benefits from the
psychotherapeutic use of movement
to promote emotional, social,
cognitive, and physical integration
of the individual, for the purpose
of improving health and well-being,
which is Dance Movement Therapy (DMT).
Thus rendering a performance platform
from which choreographerauthor's can
explore behavioral health assessment
in conjunction with clinical talk
psychotherapy treatment.

A microscope enters.

Mandating a poem piece that
intentionally intersects our mind with
the entirety of the bones and muscles of
our body as a practice of intersecting
movement with every word rendering a
kind of creativity convention that the
ideal audience must activate through a
practical practice of praxis (reflection-
healing activity-reflection-) wherein
doing reveal this self care project
fully.

Providing a look at one
choreographerauthor's short-term
utilization of techniques from DMT and
Poetry models from an ethnographic
research angle whereby praxis on
nightmares resulting from experiencing
or witnessing a traumatic event take up
space.

Contents.

Why this matters enters.
Enter you.

The Nightmare Passenger

Enter your own God. Enter words. Dance
go. Enter worthlessness feelings. Enter
the voice of the author. Enter the
sound of your own voice. Mix that, the
first, voice into socratic seminar with
the other voices present. Enter toy.
Enter cultural trade. Enter aftermath.
Enter activism. Enter results. Enter
directions. Enter grown men. Enter
action. Enter stars. Enter namesake.
Enter boss. Enter bag. Enter brag. Enter
families. Exit families. Enter families.
Exit families. Enter families. Enter
clerks. Enter coworker. Enter suicide.
Enter then. Enter again. Enter suicide
management.

Reenter Eric, Angela and John

as a visible energy that returns and
leaves in cycles. Enter in as well.
Enter in the word the. Enter in matters.
Enter your own costs. Enter colors grey,
orange and manila. Enter madagascar
vanilla. Enter gun control. Enter taxed
cigarettes. Enter and. Enter primary
sources. Enter disbelief. Enter falling.
Enter greetings. Enter hair. Enter
nephew name. Enter cousin name. Enter
priest name. Enter Post Traumatic Stress
Disorder. Enter like fighting a war
language. Gravemarker enter. Gravemarker
write the name of the reader's babe on
a gravestone. Enter more words. Enter
the colors blue, black and yellow.
Enter pockets. Enter more worthlessness
feelings. Enter capitalism. Enter as a
result of you. The root enter. Judge of
character enter. Enter animals. Exit
halloween cat. Enter untaxed cigarettes.

Enter disputed circumstances.

Enter hoodies. Enter waving actions of
hands. Enter greetings. Enter ratchets.
Enter grandmother. Enter black girls.
Enter differences. BB pellet roles in
without being asked to enter. Lazy
susan chair enters casting a shadow.
Exit concrete and yellow painted lines.
Enter fleeing. Enter running. Enter a
team of office-sized lazy susan sofas.
Enter gas smell. Enter babies. Exit
engines. Enter middle name. Enter no.
Enter oil stains. Enter babies growing
up into women. Enter given name. Enter
trans understanding. Enter surname.
Enter more worthlessness feelings. Enter
survive. Exit families. Enter families.
Exit families. Enter families. Enter
flying insects and bugs that crawl.
Enter honeybees. Enter gravemarker
write M.O.N.E.Y. on a cash box.
Enter research. Enter a body of work
indicating correlation between trauma
and suicidal behaviors. Enter Igbo
landing. Cultural competencies enter.
Enter families. Exit families. Enter
families. Enter large square tiles.
Enter feet with shoes, feet that do not
wear shoes. Enter obesity.

Enter women.

Enter them. Enter their. Enter
malnutrition. Enter males. Enter
feeling of wearing right shoes on wrong
feet. Enter self-doubt. Enter signs
plastic held together standing up with
glue, metal, shelves that are stocked
out, shelves without stock. Queer
understanding enter. Enter plastic lids.
Enter the bases they correspond. Enter
brown plastic lids. Enter the brown
bases the brown lids correspond. Enter
knowledge that each grouping of bases
and lids are different from the other.
Enter Division. Enter professional
development. Enter Diversity. Enter
knowledgeable staff. BB rolls in again.
Enter context. Eric Enter. Enter Angela.
Enter collard greens. Enter a well
securing BB container box or bag. Enter
tofurkey. Enter a cover for the lazy
susan chair. Enter blinking lights,
lights that present a sustained glow
brilliance. Enter people who gravemarker
will greet later, by name. Enter time
before present moment. Let time go by
months.

Enter dirt.

Enter flooring. Enter gravemarker, write
P.R.I.C.E.S. on sign. Enter smell of
popping corn popping. See BB out of
line. Lazy susan chair enters in a
shadow. Enter another BB box to place
the already entered BB box container
inside. Cover for the chair enter. Enter
large bags of animal food. Enter paper.
Enter large bugs that slide. Enter more
shelving. Enter advertisements. Enter
more stock. Enter names. Enter police.
Enter guns. Enter the color white. Enter
sunlight. Enter the color red. Enter
glass doors. Enter merchandise things.
Walls enter. Enter place. Enter history.
Gravemarker write U.N.B.E.A.T.A.B.L.E.L.
on one sign. Write G.E.N.D.E.R.E. across
a placard with a toilet seat drawn on
it. Write B.O.Y.S.A. on the other side
of U.N.B.E.A.T.A.B.L.E.T. Enter the
sound of footsteps. Enter tablet. Enter
background noises.

Enter people in great financial need and those with lesser need.

Enter roses. Enter trust. Enter
energy. Enter responsibility. Exit
responsibilities for others. Enter a
blue hearse entering a road. Enter
doubt. Exit doubt. Faithfulness
enter. Enter sight beyond pretexts.
Enter communion. Enter wounds. Enter
chastisement. Enter what we need. Sweet
blood of Jesus enter. Enter joy. Enter
Paul. Enter power. Enter explanation.
Enter people who are hanging upside
down. Enter a fence. Enter spiritual
sensitivity. William enter. Enter
servants. Exit leaders. Enter justice.
People enter. Enter own desires. Exit
particular eyes that are opened. Heaven
enter. Expectations of people enter.
Enter openness. Enter closed mindedness.
Exit energy. Exit conversation. Black
experience enter. Enter verdicts. Enter
academic support person. BB rolls in.
Enter employee fears. Enter adaptations.
Enter I. Enter you. Enter rooms that are
small. Enter the time it takes to get
through to the end-otherside. Enter a
BB box. Enter patience. Enter spaces to

taste free food. Enter the patience to listen.

Enter families (I).

Exit your family entirely. Enter more
words that work. Enter more faces.
Additional eyes that see enter. Enter
an effective cover for the lazy susan
chair. Enter a bad smell. Enter the
feeling when something passes you by
quickly. Enter different bodies. Exit
wheels, rolling between lines of metal
held in place. Enter frat. Enter skin.
Enter sorors. Enter spirit. Enter
shopping carts. Enter your own smell.
Enter security measures. Enter the word
lords. Exit the word sold. Gravemarker
enter something solidly sleeping. Enter
the sold word again later. Enter EGGS.
Enter knowledge that EGGS refer to the
fragility of life. Exit out safety
containers. Enter your whole family.
Exit families. Enter families. Exit
families. Enter Harriet, befuddled
watching. Enter second chances. Enter
third chances. Enter fourth chances.
Enter nightmare. Enter your dream job.
Enter families. Exit families. Enter
families. Exit families. Enter families.
Enter a snack. Enter a kick in the don't
say that language. F.U. enter. Enter a

smack in the face. Behind closed doors
enter. Enter newspapers. Enter men
and women who work everyday. Exit out
one thing that you do not think fits.
Fans that oscillate and fans that do
not move beyond where they are pointed
enter. Enter trash blowing in the wind.
Enter people who are paid well to keep
cities tidy. Enter dreams. Exit safety.
Enter in your own language. Common
sense enter. Enter people who are paid
to oppress. Enter double standards.
Enter moral dishonesty. Enter lack.
Gain enter. Enter name of the game.
Clapback enter. Enter safety. Exit safe
feelings. Enter mops. Enter books. Enter
telescope. Enter sight. Enter more
worthlessness feelings. Enter collisions
involving cars and personalities. Enter
ambulances. Enter selling cotton. Enter
slave masters. Enter supervisors. Enter
the cost of telling the truth. Enter
twelve hundred wash towels. Enter eleven
hundred containers for containing wash
towels. See 100 wash towels left without
some container. Bag enters for 50 of the
remaining wash towels. A box for 20 wash
towels enters. Enter the bin wash towels
are usually purchased in individually.

Enter lying, untruth bucket.

Exit the word usually. Enter brand name
rectangular products. Enter typical. Bad
math enter. Enter compact disks, cameras
that record bodies, body parts and,
soundscapes. Enter a BB box that works
to secure the out of line BB pellet.
Enter labels. Exit homosexuality.
Enter gay. Exit fag and dyke. Enter
eyes seeing signs. Enter yes. Enter
your own foundation garments. Enter
gravemarker write D.I.E.D. Exit cover
and lazy susan chair. Please cover
and chair exit. BB pellet please stay
in the box that is for you. Enter the
word hurt. Enter the word hunt. Enter
how. Enter how this author is feeling.
Hunted animal enter. Enter a band and a
cocktail. Remember that the sweet blood
of Jesus is entered. Enter a brand of
a bull's shit. Enter people looking at
you. Enter logic. Enter assumption.
Enter traditions. Enter medicines.
Enter mental health. Enter words tote,
prevention, vests. Gravemarker write
S.E.A.S.O.N.S. on a grey board.

Enter tombs and black dead bodies.

Enter mother's memory. Enter rocks.
Enter last words that you spoke. Enter
your own face. Enter the obituary
program. Enter yourself looking
at yourself. Enter more and more
worthlessness feelings. Exit white
pupils. Enter signs plastic held
together standing up with glue, metal,
shelves that are stocked out, shelves
without stock. Enter plastic lids that
are shorter than the brown ones. Enter
the bases that correspond to the longer
lids. Enter what happens
when things or people do not fit in.
Enter the definition of diversity. Enter
lack of support. Enter identity. Enter
abuse. Sweat enter. Enter feeling
unsafe. Enter training. Enter dismiss.
Enter fear. Enter anxieties that come
with this manner of remembering and
lived experiences.

Enter things that make fire.

Enter things that are impossible to
forget. Weed enter. Enter time some
months past a week ago. Enter the site
of your death. Exit the city you were
born. Enter more worthlessness feelings.
BB enters. Enter suicidal thoughts.
Enter in your mind's eye. Enter bacon,
tomato, bread lettuce. Enter puke. Enter
people assumed to lack home training.
Enter people assembled together.
Enter support. Enter diversity in the
workplace. Enter your own body. Enter
reasonability.

Enter police shooting John.

Enter your parent's bodies. Exit your
own body. Gravemarker write W.L.M.R.T.
on a sign. Enter the sounds and smells
of a small room where a human is kept
for 23 hours a day, for days upon days.
Enter bars that are metal. Enter where
you think that is. Enter dismissal.
Enter rooms placed in between other
small rooms separated by bars. Mouth
enters. Enter coffee. Enter containers of
water. Enter donuts. Enter spit. Enter
support staff. Enter more donuts. Enter
music. Enter caution tape acting as a
kind of paneling or concealer. Enter
body cameras. Enter sound of cameras
that click at different times. Innocence
and anyway enter. Enter heavy breathing.
Enter the solution. Enter our earthly
ages. Enter applesauce. Enter more
shelving. Enter work schedules. Enter
nickname. Enter spaces for the name you
call yourself. Enter America. Enter a
retail store. Enter more bullshit. Enter
specificity. Enter pressure. Enter your
knowledge that there aren't doors to let
this pressure out. Enter possibility.
Enter cakeboys and cheesecake. See BB

pellet out their box. Enter responses
to the wishes of others. Enter a
customer service representative. Enter
uncomfortable stress feelings. Enter the
mason dixon line. Enter bitches and male
dogs. Enter roaches that run when the
lights turn on. Enter you smoke. Enter
muzzle and seeing lines trespassed.
Enter the word bogus. Enter disrespect.
Enter the word emergency. Enter first
black university president. Enter first
black American president. Enter who
gives a phuck. Enter how many times do
I have to say it to you language. I
am scared enter. Enter the meaning of
emergency. Enter support. Daryl enter.
Daryl exit. Enter disregard. Enter not
by that brother. Enter more and more and
more and more worthlessness feelings.
Enter a lot of suicidal thoughts. Enter
fingers. Enter blood pressure rate high.
Enter blood pressure rate higher. Enter
trigger. Exit trigger. Enter bangs.
Enter hair bangs black women used to
wear in the 80's. Bridge enter. Enter
time. You enter on the bridge.

Enter someone seeking guidance.

Enter BB box we requested. Lazy susan
chair cover enters. Enter exasperation.
Enter things that lie an individual
down, on the ground, and have them
leaning up against corners. Eyeglasses
enter. Attention enter. Judge enter.
Teacups enter. Common room enter. Enter
black twisted hairs. Enter a cell
phone. Enter a ball cap. Enter a phone
call. Enter in balmoral. Gravemarker
write K.F.B. L.I.O.R. in a book. E.R.K.
A.A.D.E.W.O. must be written in the
appropriate spaces. Enter visitors.
Gravemarker write J.U.L.Y. on a stone.
Enter ivy growing where he took his
life. Enter the sound of visitors'
footsteps. Reenter into the sound of
noises that should still be in your
ear because they have been entered and
not exited out. Enter backwards. Enter
your memory. Enter rememory. Enter air
conditioning units. Enter grass in a
garden. Enter baby's breath flowers.
Enter John. Enter knowledge that this
John is not the same John previously
entered though this John is died and
gone too. Enter trust. Enter the

distinctions comprising a unique name.
Enter hence. Enter Martinez. Enter more
than enough worthlessness feelings.
Enter a different energy. Enter a kitchen
table and stuff to sit on the table.
Exit a body. Enter a hearse backing up
exiting. Enter what seems like a glowing
white coffin. Enter cremation. Enter legs
crossed but private parts still raped.
Enter progeny.

Enter semen and Exit big dicks

Ovum enter. Enter breeding bucks black.
Enter Donnie. Enter new. Enter a colored
section. Exit new energy. Enter large
male shorts. Neutered cat enter. End
enter. In enter. Sight enter. Otherwise
of black experiences enter. Enter
another coffin. Enter more not guilty
verdicts. Enter your own momma's fears.
Enter adaptations to address fear. Enter
frfr language. Enter patience. Enter
communicative words. Enter workrooms
that are hostile. Enter the same suicide
thoughts. Enter jailhouse mannerisms.
Exit patience. Enter dicks in. Enter the
time it takes to endlessly move. Exit
big dicks. Enter hunger. Enter stomach
gurgling. Enter communication. Enter
big black dick. Enter unresponsiveness.
Enter more worthlessness feelings.
Enter words that encourage. Enter your
neighbor's God. Enter one million
attempts to feel safe. Enter putting it
on your tongue. Enter negotiating for
your support. Enter one million attempts
to get help. Enter unresponsiveness.
Enter worthlessness feelings. Enter
suicide ideation. Exit families. Enter

a calculator. Enter a Tuesday. Enter
the August month. Gravemarker write
the numeral 3 on the internet. Enter
electronics. Enter the time exact she
passed away. Enter accessible doors with
handles, without handles, and, electric
doors. Enter acceptance. Enter tension.
Struggle enter. Enter Love. Historicism
enter. Enter human conditions.
Enter roadside. Gravemarker write
L.I.V.E.B.E.T.T.E.R. on a wall. Enter
chirping bird sounds out of the corner.
Enter music mixing up into chirps. Enter
rememory again. Enter your thought.
Enter empathy and critical engagement.
Enter the seventh month day. Enter time
that past quickly. Enter present time.
Enter the other John who will get shot
and later die.

Remember Angela who will collapse and later die.

Remember Angela is written with a
surname that is Williams. Remember
general. Remember generational
designations. Remember John is written
with a surname that is Crawford. Enter
a supermarket. Enter in seconds. Enter
ink. Gravemarker write generational
designation (III or the third) on
paper behind name John Crawford. Enter
garments for attending a funeral. Enter
diverse bodies who will celebrate in
those clothes. Enter Oh'happyday lyrics.
Exit hearses past coffins. Enter gold.
Enter desperation. Enter expectation.
Exit a crowd pleaser. Enter a good beat
tho. Exit families.

Enter blessings. Enter humming. Enter
ownership. Enter America. Enter scared
to open the door. Enter worship. Enter
to walls being built. Move death's
standing next to scared and to. Enter
scared to death. Enter intimidation.
Enter at work. Exit things that
belong to them. Enter more things
you personally need. Enter equality.

Enter crying. Enter another ask for
support. Enter unresponsiveness. Enter
providers. Enter degree credentials.
Enter more worthlessness feelings. Enter
intimidation. Enter unresponsiveness is
typical. Enter great resources. Enter
paper on the floor. Enter what a God can
do. Enter a land surrounded by water.
Isolation enter. Bridge to what is next
enter. Enter rivers running deep.

Love enter. Enter island. Enter Ti Moune
characteristic.

Enter preparation for burial.

Enter Erzulie.

Enter sea. Enter sheol. Enter fashion.
Enter sagging pants. Exit fashion.
Enter your rights. Agwé enter. Wrapping
waves enter. Enter sweet smelling
perfume. Enter time that is closer to
an end. Enter cold. Enter fatalities.
Enter gravemarker. Enter decomposition
process. Enter heat. Enter bed sheets
ripped. Enter nightmares. Enter
assignments. Enter families. Exit
families. Enter the seashore. Enter
Papa Ge. Enter debate. Enter risk.
Enter love. Enter being carried to
shore. Enter psychological distress.
Enter suicide in trauma survivorship.
Enter being wrapped by waves. Enter
a human turned into a tree. Enter
recycling. Enter a pact to enter into
real love. Enter a noose rope tie.
Enter some studies. Enter suggestions.
Enter intimidation. Enter a body bag.
Enter success. Enter boundaries to
it. Borderlines enter. Enter more
worthlessness feelings. Enter ignore.
Skeletons enter. Enter intimidate. Enter
a comment posting. Enter ignorant. Enter
physical illness. Closet enter.

Enter different electronics (I).

Enter less time than you think. Enter
forever. Enter wheelchair accessible
doors with handles, without handles,
electric and ramps. Enter more pressure.
Struggles heightened enter. Enter
acceptance speeches. Love heightened
enter. Enter another road. Gravemarker
write enter. Handhold to breasts enter.
Asaka enter. Gravemarker speak near
Dayton settlement location. Gravemar...
Gravemarker speak numerals 2.0.1.4.
Enter movement restrictions. Gravemarker
welcome sad, sad mothers. Enter time
before december month. Gravemarker
take time, write numeral 4 on the
internet in a manner that will stay.
Enter family friends. Enter chirping
bird sounds out of tree branches by
gravestones and mausoleums. Enter
survivor's tears. Enter bird's music
mixing up and out into death ritual
songs. Enter someone you know, love and
need to forgive. Enter hard to remember
faces and sound of their voices. Enter
the thoughts and feelings of coming
and going. Remember Angela who will
collapse and later die. Remember

Angela is written with a surname that
is Williams. Enter another person
named John Crawford. Do not get these
confused. Enter additional education on
distinguishing factors like generational
designations and namespaces. Enter
the Bronx borough. Enter survivors of
abuse. Enter insecurity. Enter humanity.
Enter victims. Enter feeling safe at
home. Exit safe feeling. Enter your
own protection. Enter your own manner
of protest. Enter your prejudices.
Gravemarker write E.R.I.C.G.A.R.N.E.R.T.
Across from that, in the appropriate
spaces, write R.E.S. Enter more garments
for attending funerals.

**Enter neck, wrist and ankle shackles
then Enter people who do their job.**

Enter families. Enter fresh flowers.
Enter guilty. Enter wayment language.
Enter criminals. Enter doing it for
the money attitudes. Enter you do not
know me language. Enter your own mind.
Enter burdens laid down. Enter more
pockets. Enter time closer to an end but
not justice. Enter courthouses. Enter
systems causing deaths. Enter systems
supporting people. Enter no worries. No
stress enter. Enter stable living. Enter
peace of mind. Enter Akeem. Enter house.
Enter window shades lifting. Enter
growing ivy at Kalief's bedroom window.
Enter people who do their job. Enter
commodity.

Enter acknowledgment. Enter not wanting
to die. Enter choose. Choice enter.
Enter a new kind of intimidation. Enter
another wall. Enter people who build
walls. Enter a different orange. Enter
tired. Exit sleep. Enter hurting heads.
Enter scholarship. Enter intellectual
minds under hoodies. Enter babies
with brighter futures. Exit birthday.

Enter Raheem. Enter Venida. Enter
Deion. Enter entering. Exit Venida and
Kalief in a reverse order than their
names are written here. Enter more
worthlessness feelings and thoughts.
Enter discernment on innocence. Enter
those going through the same things.
Enter protestors. Enter fair use. Help
enter. Enter sandals. Enter holding
yourself together. Enter your best
light. Enter closed-toed shoes. Enter
suspenders. Enter having to urinate.
Enter pens. Enter broach like a subject.
Enter clothes adorned by brooches.
Enter concrete rubbing against cheeks,
knuckles, elbows, knees, and backs
of bodies that are generally read as
black, bodies without as much melanin or
soul, real or putative. Enter handcuffs.
Enter the wrists they correspond. Enter
a reversal. Enter more contexts. Enter
chests. Enter chokeholds. Enter Daniel.
Enter Muhammad. Enter martyrs. Enter
upside down perspective. Enter sources.
Enter Hebrew. Letting time go by months
that make years enter. Enter books.
Enter selfies. Enter recordings. Enter
labor unions. Enter associations. Enter
phones. Enter proof.

Enter recording a stoop.

Gravemarker write H.T.T.P.S.Y.O.U.T.
U.B.E.B.E.Z.J.L. on a world wide web
page. Include standard punctuation
marks and numbers. Enter backslash,
backslash, colon ,dash, 7,0,0,9,4,0.
at the correct places in order to
make a web address. Enter remembering
discernment of innocence. Gravemarker
write W.H.A.T.D.I.D.I.D.O. on a line.
Enter the smell of gunpowder. Remember
he can't breath. Enter legal counsel
representation. Enter except he is
already dead. Sounds of choking enter.
Enter numbers 9 and 9 placed together on
a shirt. Enter a stoop. Enter I ain't
doing nuttin' language. Enter powdered
donuts. Enter persons who listen.
Enter more shelves. Enter deals. Enter
news coverage. Enter other survivors.
Enter throats. Enter rubber bands.
Enter rubber gloves. Enter degrees.
Enter edges. Exit families. Exit more
families.

Enter families (II).

Enter mom. Enter one of mom's
kids. Enter a grocery store. Enter
repercussions of being born into a
system. Enter an edge. Exit mom.
Exit one of mom's kids. Enter family
reunification. Gravemaker see over an
edge but do not speak or write what
you see. Enter help. Enter ears to
hear. Enter more witnesses. Enter
characteristics from other art. Enter
hosts Angelou Maya talked about. Rock,
River and Tree speaking enter. Enter
their message. Enter education. Enter
on the pulse of morning language. Enter
titles. Gravemarker greet the Asian,
the Hispanic, the Jew, the African,
the Native American, the Sioux, the
French, the Greek, the Turk, the Swede,
the German, the Eskimo, the Scot, the
Ashanti, the Yoruba, the Kru, bought,
sold, stolen, arriving on a nightmare
praying for a dream. Gravemarker greet
the Irish, the Rabbi, the Priest, the
Sheikh, the Gay, the Straight, the
Preacher, the Privileged, the Homeless,
the Catholic, the Muslim, the Teacher,
the Pawnee, the Apache, the Seneca,

the Cherokee Nation, who rested with
the hosts then forced on bloody feet—.
Gravemarker ask those characteristics'
bodies if they would bare their souls
as witnesses in their own ways. Enter
a can of worms. Exit that can's lid.
Enter more shelving. Enter appropriate
names for people. Enter more stock.
Enter postage stamps sent through
general human trafficking mail and stamps
showcasing only variously at collections
in book materials. Enter chinaware
shops. Enter horses in the chinaware
shops. Enter issues. Exit horses. Glass
everywhere enter. Enter duh language.
Enter another chinaware shop. Enter
bulls. Enter moonlight. Enter twilight
time. Enter glass doors. Enter what
happened when the horses were in the
chinaware shop. Enter duh language
again. Enter glass everywhere again.
Enter a day. Enter the August month.
Gravemarker write the figure 5 on the
internet again.

Enter different electronics (II).

35 whatsoevers enter inhaling. Enter
time. Enter inheritance. Enter or
else. Enter doors with handles,without
handles, manually manipulated. Enter
alone feelings. Enter tension. Struggle
entering bitterness enter. Love turning
towards lust enter. Historic languages
enter. Human conditions of oppression
enter. Enter roadside assistance.
Enter talented man killed too soon.
Gravemarker write L.O.W. Enter near
Dayton settlement but specifically at
Englewood location. Enter chirping
bird sounds out of the ceiling again.
Enter your own music mixing up into the
chirps of birds. Enter memory again.
Enter thought again. Enter more and
more gunshots. Enter yelling. Enter
empathy and critical engagement. Enter
projects. Do not forget Angela who
will collapse and later die. Remember
Angela is written with a surname that
is Williams. Enter the eleventh month
day. Enter too much time past. Enter
Mellissa who presumably committed
suicide after leaving work at The Ohio
State University. Enter the soul of

the boy who was killed on campus at
The Ohio State University. Remember
the author was arrested while sitting
down in a waiting room at The Ohio
State University. Enter present
time. Enter another John. Enter in
seconds. Enter why not. Enter lack
of trust. Enter truly hearing. Enter
your knowledge. Enter forgetting that
experience. Enter phone conversations.
Enter learning more. Gravemarker write
A.C.C.O.U.N.T. in the air. Enter
different color garments for attending
funerals. Enter diverse bodies to stand
and celebrate in those clothes. Enter
Oh'happyday flowers. Exit the hearses.
Enter things you can't explain. Enter
more walls. Enter a new place. Enter
stillness. Enter the mindset there is
no place else to go. Gravemarker write
U.N.I.V.E.R.S.I.T.Y. on one sign. Write
H.O.O.I. near U.N.I.V.E.R.S.I.T.Y. in
another order rendering proper credits.
Enter the sound of footsteps. Enter
intimidation and disparities. Lazy susan
chair enters again. BB pellet enters on
a platform. Enter a cover for the chair
and container for the out of line BB on
the platform. Enter back in and out all
of the things that have come and gone.
Enter gon' through some things language.
Enter a-many-of open doors. Enter
staying a while. Shirt buttons enter.

Enter additional body parts.

Enter blood donors. Enter psychological
responses to traumatic events, abuses
and mediators. Enter crackers, cookies
with white cream in the middle of black
baked enclosures and a cheese puff snack.
Enter ham sandwiches. Enter a pocketbook
or purse. Enter numbers that do not
lie. Exit hair. Enter barbers who cut
hair in people's homes. Exit energy.
Enter racism. Exit conversation. More
of everything you need enter. Enter
short-haired citizens, citizens with
longer hair, and citizens who wear hoods
that are different from the hoodie kind.
Enter bigots. Enter anthem spangled.
Enter a banner with stars on it. Enter
things that come to the surface in a
dream. Enter hearing white folx calling
your name out. Enter criminal record.
Enter joblessness. Enter sense of
humor. Enter needing socks, soap and
toothpaste. Enter fantastic. Enter
smells of burning flesh. Enter a sense
of imagination if you do not know what
flesh burning smells like. Enter not
good. Enter who wit me language. Enter
who you wit language. Enter anger. Enter

strangers and strangeness. Enter pills.
Enter on. Enter enter. Enter different
pants pockets. Enter different levels
of anxiety. Enter teenagers that sell
baseball cards. Enter folx who sell
makeup. Enter more frozen food items.
Enter fresh pink meat.

Alexander Nmoma
Podiatrist

CHN 235 255
E Houston St

Tel 212 477-1120
Fax 212 477 8957

Enter thoughts that meat are negros.

Enter the smell of fish rotting. Enter
rotting fish being thrown away. Open
your own mouth. Enter your own child.
Open someone else's mouth. Remember
reading signs that read this way. Enter
strange wind. Enter families. Exit
families. Enter families. Exit families.
Enter hymn. Enter uniforms. Enter so.
Enter why. Enter not. Enter you. Enter
mess. Enter good. Enter loyalty. Enter
royalties. Enter traditional way of
doing things. Enter paranormal action.
Enter knowing what you do. Enter sex.
Beauty stay. Ugly have limits. Again,
beauty stay, ugly limit yourself. Enter
bad that is perceived to be good. Enter
Russell. Enter Thelma. Enter staplers.
Enter coats. Enter jewelry. Enter a new
set of annoyances. 200 subtract 101
problems enter.

Enter job applications.

Exit the word yes. Enter self doubt.
Enter doubt that is on the outside of
yourself. Enter knowledge that doubt
feelings deal with worthlessness
thoughts. Enter untalented. Enter
unbelievable. Enter entered. Murder
to excellence enter. Enter having to
explain. Enter there are no words
language. Exit rest. Exit thriving. BB
and lazy Susan chair enter together
again. Enter retaliatory situation.
Coursework enter. Enter oh' no you
didn't language. Enter prayer oil. Enter
pillows. Exit comfort. Enter mentorship.
Enter let me think about that and get
back to you language.

Enter clock.

Ticking enter. Enter enter again.
Enter unresponsiveness. Enter publish
or perish language. Enter everyone
else knows things kept away from you.
Enter current societies. Enter dance
scholarship. Exit respect for the
work you do. Enter pioneers. Exit
encouragement for some people. Enter
psychological responses to trauma,
abuses, oppression, mismanagement and
same old same old shit. Enter death
threats at school to black gyrls and
black students. Enter not this again
language. Enter fighting the same war
on another front. Enter transatlantic
slavery with trademark money. Enter
colloquialism. Feces enter. Enter jimmy
crow. Enter when exactly is enough
enough language. Enter pallbearers.
Enter flames for cremation and embalming
fluid for the wake and casket resting.
Injections enter. BB pellet exits.

Enter I shit you not language. BB pellet
enters again. See BB out of place,
again. Enter that is just the way it
is language. Chair that is lazy enters

making a shadow. Enter truthfulness of
responsibility. Enter an additional
box for BB pellet. Enter appropriate
lighting to shed light on shadowy chair.

Enter the missing periods.

Gravemarker sleep. Enter results of
living nightmares. Woke up.

Recent Titles from Unlikely Books.

Political AF: A Rage Collection by Tara Campbell

The Deepest Part of Dark by Anne Elezabeth Pluto

Swimming Home by Kayla Rodney

Manything by dan raphael

Citizen Relent by Jeff Weddle

The Mercy of Traffic by Wendy Taylor Carlisle

Cantos Poesia by David E. Matthews

Left Hand Dharma: New and Selected Poems by Belinda Subraman

Apocalyptics by C. Derick Varn

Pachuco Skull with Sombrero: Los Angeles, 1970 by Lawrence Welsh

Monolith by Anne McMillen (Second Edition)

When Red Blood Cells Leak by Anne McMillen (Second Edition)

My Hands Were Clean by Tom Bradley (Second Edition)

anonymous gun. by Kurtice Kucheman (Second Edition)

Soy solo palabras but wish to be a city by Leon De la Rósa, illustrated by Gui.ra.ga7 (Second Edition)

Police
212 477 7811

Christine
646 510 7106

VV 212 717 2838
POLICE